CROCHET FOR ABSOLUTE BEGINNERS:

THE ESSENTIAL GUIDE TO CROCHETING YOUR VERY FIRST PROJECT IN LESS THAN 2 HOURS. INCLUDES SUPER EASY PATTERNS TO RELAX WHILE SPENDING YOUR FREE TIME PRODUCTIVELY

By Sarah Afghan

Table of Contents

Introduction

Crochet is an embroidery method that utilizes a crochet hook with fiber or similar material. This fiber is most usually wool or crochet thread, but it could also be leather, rope, twine, or other inventive content.

Crochet fans are looking forward to finishing crochet creations that are usually useful, desirable, or helpful items somehow. Common initiatives typically involve Afghans, crocheted blankets, baby booties, sweaters, beanies, and squares of granny, shawls, pouches, tote bags, and many others. Several different things can be crocheted, including brooches, socks, and curtains.

It is also important to use different components in other products to crochet. Crochet trims as well as edgings, for example, are common projects; you may add them to crocheted products, knitted items, as well as sewn pieces (including ready-made shop-bought items), such as purchasing some shoes, towels, and pillowcases, and applying a crocheted finish to each.

Crochet is a form of craft in which a small hooked needle or rod is used along with yarn to create items or sheets of fabric with different textures and appearances through using different techniques.

The main differences between crochet and knitting are the types of stitches and the techniques used. For instance, knitting incorporates using two same size needles at the same time to work the wool and create sheets of fabric at a time. With crochet, you only use a single needle at one time as well as your hands. That also means you only have one active stitch at a time, whereas in knitting, you have many active stitches at any one time, making it easier to drop a stitch without noticing accidentally.

Crochet is also remarkably easier to pick up over knitting; crochet has very simple beginner stitches which you can use even in the early stages of learning to create cute and funky little objects. It is a great encouragement for a beginner to see their hard work begin to grow and take shape in front of them.

Chapter 1. Crochet History

No one knows when or how crochet has been made. It's because, instead of knitting, crochet was the artwork, rather than the advanced lace knitting produced for the Royalty and the upper class and eventually preserved for study in museums and historians.

Over the years, crochet has been more transparent than knitting needles and more flexible to make more fun and inventive clothing, shoes, Afghans, and much more.

Historians assume that the lower classes invented Crochet.

It left someone who wanted luck in a sport and was evil. But when these textiles were made available to the new middle class, they were used mostly for knitting darn socks.

An informal crochet movement started with people who could find a few strands or threads and then decorative knots and chains using their fingers. This initial attempt was probably similar to macramé instead of crochet but was still a cheap and revolutionary art.

The people of Turkey, Persia, North Africa, China, and India may have started to make iron, bone, ivory, and wood hooks around the 1300s. But before people began to "crochet in the air," as it was later called in France in the 1800s, there first evolved another type of knots and loops.

Since no one understood that the crochet stitch could produce a garment on its own, it turned to a technique known as' tambouring.' This method was first developed in China and included crochet-like stitches created from textiles.

It was roughly 1700 that textile manufacturers stretched out a background material taught to frame and then passed the thread loop through the material using a crochet needle. The hook was combined into the first chain point when the next loop was created.

By the mid-1700s, there were enough tambourine pieces from the East to inspire Europeans to practice tambourine art.

Finally, the fabric was removed, and the first modern crochet was created using hooks made from silver, brass, or steel by the Europeans, who learned to drum. Once upon a time, only the upper class could crochet who inspired the masses to start drinking their socks and dream of more creative outlets.

However, it was time that people learned to make their hooks and adorn their garments with odds and ends of the fabric. (The crochets were used for the first time in Europe to create whole clothing and decorate existing clothing) The upper class, who made crochet fashionable, saw and proclaimed it out of fashion, the growing middle class and its new crochet immediately.

Then the knits left, the lower classes couldn't afford, and just left to crochet until the queen Victoria took crochet and make it fashionable again.

Although a more modern crochet version was born in Italy and Spain, the French developed the crochet in the late 1700s, naming it from the middle French word crochet or crochet knot. Throughout this time, crocheted lace was also made.

Later, standardized patterns that were easy to follow were circulated. When standard needles were made, crochet in the middle of the 1800s became the most inexpensive way for the growing middle class to spend time on the fire and make unique clothes, accessories, and home decorations.

Modern crochet remains the needle-based art of people to this day. It is easy to understand, fun to do, and much less restrictive than its knitting relatives.

I'm aware of a few crochet types, the most commonly used, called, in the West, crochet, which involves various methods, using yarn and loop stitches; terms such as slip stitch, chain stitch, double crochet stitch, half and triple stitch and more.

Archeological findings suggest that Arabia could be the first place where a needle and hook worked cloth. Ancient findings from Egypt indicate skilled use of the needles and hooks from 950BC-1200BC.

Throughout its long history, crochet is a word from the French word "croc" which means "hook" and is believed to be employed by men and women.

A technique that can be used while sitting, standing or in motion; using a variety of yarn, linen, cotton, silk, and wool, including precious metal finely beaten and golden spun, to manufacture garments, jewelry, bags, tapestries, tissue to cover furniture has been used in the Middle East for thousands of years.

Is it Tunisian crochet, or is it Afghan or Tricot crochet?

Where and when the first surface appears like a cross between a hook and a needle.

Was it Tunisian? A crochet type that can look like crochet, knitting, or weaving was the leading man of these fabrics?

Slip crochet stitch, maybe the earliest crochet and fabric type.

Broom-stick crochet is also known as peacock lace; where and where did this come from?

Was it the founder of Europeans who traveled around the USA in covered wagons, had bulbs and hooks, got the expertise, brought them from their homeland, needed very warm bedding and clothing, began to create a fast and simple crochet style?

Irish crochet, traditional Irish crochet, 3D luxury lace characteristic of a net of picots (called fillers), ladies, romantic and beautiful, with its crocheted petals, flowers, and leaves.

A subgroup called 'baby Irish crochet' in Irish crochet is continuously working in squares or circular sections. In the 1870s, crochet was the salvation of many Irish families by making 12,000 to 20,000 crochet lace for their families during the years of the potato famine and beyond.

Bruges Crochet, a lace made in trebles and chain stitch, the crochet bands are combined to make a lace-like transparent string.

Bavarian Crochet, new to me, this regional crochet is something I need to know.

Aran crochet is like knitting Aran; it shapes a fabric with elevated areas from a flat backdrop.

Filet crochet was very common in the 1920s and 1950s and is famous due to the simple mesh structure and patterns in the lace; it's easy using Hairpin Crochet Charts, supposedly made in the Queen Victorian period by women using their hairpins and hooks to make a modern type of crochet that is used in linear and fine circular laces.

Today, we have replaced the pins with looms that are easily adjustable in size to make working this crochet shape easier.

Revival in the '60s as individuals began to make modern design garments by hand in non-compliant shapes and colors to the day's standards.

Stripes, jacquards, patchwork, lace, fabric, hoops, knit, beaded, circles, rings, today scrumbling, crochet is a living art, reinvented and used differently infinite ways using modern materials.

Ways across history and the world have permitted people to fulfill their personal needs, earn money, feed their families, clothe themselves and their families, learn new things, and meet their needs.

Crochet in the early 21st century finds that its revival is new in manufacture, thousands of fashion and decorative products made, as well as in the hands of individuals who reveal old designs, designs new patterns and applications, handcrafted decorative objects, personal clothing and work of art.

Crochet styles are changing, and Crochet is going to live on. A modern textile craftsman; work with beautiful materials; Australia Superfine Merino, Merino, Alpaca, Angora plus, Silks, Cashmere, acrylic, floating, beads; and wearable works. Gayle Lorraine Designs by Gayle Lorraine Ancient techniques meet contemporary conceptions; East meets West, color, line, texture, and balance, important in fine art and sculpture, whether work is 1,2 3D.

Gayle paints on canvas and felt, wearable felt, Nuno, Calamari and Cobweb felt, yarns, buttons, Tunisian (Tricot, Afghani), crochet breadstick, and a little Irish crochet, and a ton of simple crochet.

Chapter 2. Crochet Supplies

Crochet Hook: The first device you need is a crochet needle. Crochet designs indicate the scale of the hooks you need to use. Your boss will help you determine which hooks to use for your first job.

Scissors: Hold a convenient pair of scissors or tweezers for thread clipping, pump cutting, etc. In a protection situation, make sure to maintain scissors.

Yarn: Yarns can be found in a multitude of weights (strand diameter) as well as fiber material. Employ the yarn indicated in the guidance for the best outcomes.

Make sure to buy all of the yarn you want for a design simultaneously, as loads of dye will differ somewhat in coloring, shown on the completed project.

Gauge: This is the number of stitches per inch (and spaces), as well as a couple of rows for every inch. Gauge is defined in many designs above four inches. Your scale will be the same as the gauge defined in the template so that your project is the right size. That's particularly important for initiatives that need to match.

Think about making a gauge palette again once you start the design. Utilize the same thread, needle, and template stitch set out in the directions to test the strength. Create a swatch of around 6 inches long. Workaround 6 inches in sequence, then attach. And let all the swatch settle a little, then squish it to fit without no stretching.

Use sticks, map off a 4-inch square segment of stitching in the middle of the swatch. Count the number of stitches as well as rows in this segment of 4 inches. Ye can start immediately on your design if they fit the scale.

If you've had very few stitches, you're operating too loose— shifting to a small hook and creating another swatch. If you've got just so many stitches, you're working too closely— shifting to a bigger hook.

Continue to make swatches as well as play with hook measurements until you get the required gauge. Different manner, everyone/crochets should help you create a design that suits you. Each yarn skein has the size of the yarn and the label's suggested hook. For your future, you'll want to retain the sticker.

Threads are used to knit as well. Crochet yarn is commonly used as a projecting edge for dollies, placemats, or tabletops. A thread of 10 dimensions is the most widely used.

The greater the number of loops, the better the thread, so finer than 10 is 20, and finer than 20 is 30. You're going to need to use a thread snare to crochet this sort. With a 10-thread dimension, a "0" hook tends to work well.

Tapestry Needle: For embroidery seams, a blunt spotted sculpture needle is used. It is safer to have a simple, steel needle. Many needles throughout the tapestry have a ridge around the neck.

These aren't perfect for crocheting seams when the hump traps stitches, making it difficult to pull through the thread.

Measuring Tools: You would need a ruler (6 or 12 inches), a tape, or a metal-measuring gauge to measure.

Hooks

We've already stated that the sizes of hooks vary from thin to thick. The skinny metal hooks are used with the best cotton yarn, but the larger ones are used for heavy wools and artificial fibers.

Hooks are made of metallic, aluminum, bone, or plastic.

When doing an assignment from a pattern, the one who wrote the sample will advocate a hook length. However, you need to be a better choice of what hook to use. Use the only one you're maximum comfortable with and the only one that will help you attain the proper gauge for a pattern.

As you go together with your work, you can need to trade hooks greater than once. The important element while choosing a hook brand is to go along with the only one you figure nicely with, and that feels good to your hand. Crocheting fans purchase their hooks based on the subsequent factors: hand length, finger length, the hook's weight, and preference for aluminum or plastic.

There is not any constant formulation for selecting the proper size hook. Remember that crocheters are distinctive. Some like to crochet tightly, a few loosely, so that this makes it tough to decide a component. Use gauge as the important thing attention – what number of stitches you want to do to make an inch.

As the professionals say, exercise makes ideal. Experimenting is even better. If you're using a plastic hook for a selected assignment and you're having problems, transfer above to an aluminum hook and spot how that feels. In time, you'll choose your favorites and understand which sizes or types provide you with high-quality effects with a nice feel.

Afghan Hook

You may also have heard of the Afghan hook that's used for specialized crochet initiatives. The Afghan hook changed into devised so that you can keep many stitches at the hook concurrently. If the average duration of a hook is six inches, this doesn't give you a lot of area.

The Afghan hook was invented to make your lifestyle easier. It is plenty longer than your normal crochet hook and is available in 3 lengths: 9-inch, 14-inch, and 20-inch. It also has knobs on the ends to preserve stitches from falling off.

And way too smart inventors, you may find a few Afghan hooks which have lengthy, bendy cords on one quit. These cords are to keep additional stitches so you can relax your paintings in your lap without the need to worry.

More About Yarns!

Regarding yarns, they're produced through spinning different varieties of fibers collectively.

The yarn industry has blended and paired fibers collectively to provide you with various sizes and textures to meet state-of-the-art crocheters' demands. Generally, the easiest yarn to paintings with is a smooth surface and a medium or tight twist for an amateur.

Yarns are offered by way of weight rather than via period. They are typically packaged into balls. The most commonplace ball size is 1-three/four oz (50 g), and the duration of every yarn will vary depending on the thickness and fiber composition.

Wool is a superb yarn to crochet with because it is stretchable, making it clean to push the hook factor into each stitch. Silk yarn is every other good for crocheting but has much less resilience than wool and is a lot extra pricey.

Synthetic fiber yarns, alternatively like acrylic, nylon, and polyester, are made from coal and petroleum products, regularly made to resemble fibers.

Yarns made of artificial fibers are less high-priced, and their advantages include stability, washing gadget-protection, and non-shrinkage. The best downside is they generally tend to lose their shape while uncovered to warmness. A better alternative might be to buy yarn, a part of artificial, element herbal fiber.

While there are common types of yarns based on weight, severe producers in severe nations will produce yarns that don't fall in the yarn's not unusual weight parameters. Here are the most acquainted ones which might be sold:

- ☐ Extra-cumbersome,
- ☐ Bulky,
- ☐ Aran wool,
- ☐ Worsted,
- ☐ Recreation,
- ☐ Aran cotton,
- ☐ Double knitting,
- ☐ Game mercerized cotton,
- ☐ Worsted acrylic
- ☐ Viscose rayon,
- ☐ Linen/viscose,
- ☐ Metal viscose,
- ☐ Steel.

While we said hook and yarn are all you want to begin crochet, other tools will substantially make your work simpler and more efficient. Here are the "extras" you'll need to maintain reachable.

Markers

Split rings or fashioned loops product of colorful plastic could mark those locations on your work in case you're working with a pattern; they indicate the beginning of a row and help in counting the stitches on the muse chain;

Tapestry Needles

These are gadgets with blunt factors and lengthy eyes and are generally used in embroidery. They varied in length and are used to weave yarn ends and for sewing crochet pieces collectively. You may also need to have a ramification of needles with sharp points for making use of crochet braid, edging, or borders.

Pins

For blockading duties, the first-rate pins are those who have a tumbler head and are rustproof. Plastic or pearl headed pins are top for pinning crochet. Quilters' lengthy pins are also ideal for pinning portions of crochet together because the heads are seen and did not win slip through the crochet fabric.

Tape Measure

Choose a tape measure that has both inches and centimeters at the equal aspect. Above time, tape measures tend to stretch, so they want to get replaced to obtain size accuracy. A plastic or metallic ruler (12 inches/30 cm) is also a very good concept to measure gauge swatches.

Row Counter

That will assist you in preserving the song of the number of rows you've got crocheted up to now; others prefer a pocketbook and pencil.

Sharp scissors – small, pointed ones are true for trimming yarn and yarn ends.

Plastic Rings

These function foundations for making buttons. Metals jewelry for button foundations isn't encouraged because they could rust while the garment is washed.

It is the most effective tool a good way to let you know the size of your hook. Don't depend upon the dimensions stamped at the hook, and constantly look at your hook's size with a steel gauge.

Bobbins

These can keep small quantities of yarns. They're an extraordinary assist while doing multi-colored paintings. Store your yarns in a secure place in which they did not get stained. A huge, smooth pillowcase might serve this purpose. When no longer in use, bundle your hooks together with a string or rubber band and maintain them in case like a beauty bag or a strong container.

The Right Material

There are a variety of materials that are suitable for crocheting. For the selection, it is important what you want to work on. So, we find the finest yarns for lace doilies up to the thick wool or the raffia for a carpet. For example, linen yarn is suitable for lace doilies, filet crochet yarn for curtains, medium cotton yarn for window curtains and crochet pillows, carpet yarn for floor carpets various cotton yarns in different strengths for many other ideas.

In addition to wool, bast or cord are also used for rough crochet work, especially for floor carpets, shopping nets, bags, and similar coarse-meshed work. However, as crocheting is the most commonly used wool, we will give you a little information on the product on the following pages. Incidentally, cotton yarn crochet patterns are most beautifully smooth to advantage because here, the musters' structure is particularly evident.

In addition to the crochet material such as yarn, bast, etc., we only need a crochet hook to crochet.

Yarns are often grouped under the term "wool," although many yarns do not contain any "real" wool from animals. Spun fiber strands (so-called "wires") of one or more fiber types are turned into a long thread of the yarn production's desired thickness. Depending on the type of fiber (s) used and how the yarn is spun and twisted, yarns with different properties are produced.

If a yarn is twisted strongly, it is firm and smooth and results in a more durable crochet piece. Loosely twisted yarn is softer to the touch but tends to be less durable. The fibers used in yarn can be of animal origin (new wool, angora, mair, silk, alpaca, and cashmere), of vegetable origin (cotton, linen, bamboo), or chemical, i.e., of synthetic origin (polyacrylic, polyester, microfiber).

Natural fibers are combined with synthetic fibers. That results in yarns that combine the skin-friendly properties of natural fibers with the durability of synthetic fibers. The percentage of the different fibers is indicated on the banderole of the yarn. If a yarn consists of only one type of fiber, this can be recognized by the statement "100%" (e.g., "100% cotton") or "pure" (e.g., "pure new wool").

Cotton is a natural fiber that is extracted from the cotton plant. Long-fiber cotton is considered to be of high quality. The best cotton quality with the longest fibers is the Egyptian "Mako cotton", which is often used in slightly more expensive yarns. Cotton is very absorbent and is, therefore, often worn in summer. Unlike synthetic fibers, however, it dries relatively slowly. Cotton is also considered a particularly skin-friendly and non-allergic material.

Linen is extracted from the fibers of the flax plant. For a time, linen was almost completely ousted by cotton, but in increasing environmental and environmental orientation in society, the fiber is gaining in importance again. Linen is a smooth, low-fluff, and dirt-repellent fiber. It can absorb a lot of moisture and has a cooling effect in the summer. Linen is very wear-resistant and durable but relatively crease-prone. In the case of needlework yarns, it usually occurs as a component of yarn.

The microfibers are a collective term for particularly thin synthetic fibers. For example, they are half as thin as silk fibers and only a quarter as thin as fine virgin wool fibers. Microfibers are very soft, extremely resistant to deformation, windproof, water-repellent, and quick drying. Due to their special wearing and care properties, they have experienced a tremendous upswing in the textile sector in recent years, not only in the case of handmade yarn but also in sportswear.

Polyacrylic, polyester, and polyamide are synthetic fibers made from synthetic materials. They are very tear-resistant and scuff-resistant, easy to care for, elastic, and crease-resistant. However, they absorb little moisture, so many people perceive them as unpleasant on the skin in their pure form. Synthetic fibers are often mixed with natural yarns such as virgin wool or cotton (the so-called Misch yarns) to make them more durable. Misch yarns are especially popular with crafting fans.

Silk is originally from China and is extracted from the silkworm's cocoons, the silk moth's larva. The noble, higher-priced fiber with the typical silky shine is fine and soft, yet firm. When dry, it is also wrinkle-free and is characterized by a high-color brilliance and wearing comfort.

Viscose, a widely used and popular fiber in the textile industry, occupies an intermediate position. It is produced in a chemical process but consists of natural raw materials (especially cellulose, increasingly, bamboo) and, therefore, it has similar skin-friendly properties as natural yarns.

Wool consists of the fur and hair of mammals such as sheep, goats, rabbits, etc. Accordingly, different types of wool are distinguished in yarns:

- **Sheep's Wool** (New Wool)

Sheep's wool is a resilient, colorfast fiber and a good thermal insulator. It only slightly dissipates the body heat, so it is worn more in the cooler season. Unlike synthetic fibers, it does not absorb much odor. Sheep wool tends to lint (pilling), which can be reduced by special processing and anti-pilling equipment. Without special equipment, coarse wool can scratch the skin uncomfortably. The wool of the Merino sheep with very good wearing properties is considered especially fine. By a chemical treatment, virgin wool can be made machine-washable. Popular among hand workers is the combination of virgin wool with a synthetic fiber, which significantly increases the yarn's durability.

- **Mohair**

Mohair is the African goat living in Asia Minor, Southern Russia, South Africa, and North America. It is white, shiny, and long-fibered. The particularly fine and high-quality hair of the young goats is called Kid-Mohair.

- **Angora**

Angora comes from the Angora rabbit and is especially soft and fluffy.

- **Alpaca**

The wool of alpaca, one camel type living in South America, keeps the heat reserved many times better in the body than sheep's wool. She is especially soft and well-suited.

- **Cashmere**

The cashmere goat is mainly native to the Himalayas. Its exceptionally fine, lightweight, and heat-insulating wool is one of the most expensive fibers ever and is often blended with virgin wool.

Tips for Buying Yarn

Yarns are not only available today from specialist retailers but also innumerable internet-shops and even discounters. If you do not have much experience with crocheting, you should buy your material there, where you can receive expert advice. Often, it is the case that you do not receive the original yarn specified in the model instruction in the trade and must switch to another yarn. Trained sales personnel can then choose a similar yarn and matching crochet hooks and other aids.

Yarns are usually sold wrapped like a ball of yarn. Common are balls with a weight of 50 grams, but sometimes, larger balls of 100 grams or more are available. In particular, very thick yarns are sometimes sold in strands. These must be wrapped in a ball before you can start crocheting.

Each ball of yarn is provided with a banderole containing various information about the yarn:

- the weight of the ball

- the composition of the yarn (percentage of individual fibers)

- the needle size recommended for the yarn

- Instructions for the care of the yarn (washability, etc.)

- The number of the hue and the color lot

For a crochet work, use only yarn of a single-color lot because only the same color lot balls are identical in color. Color deviations between balls of different color parts are usually only on the finished crochet piece.

Even if you are done with the crochet, you should always keep the banderole together with a yarn piece. So, you can always read the care instructions and always have a little bit of yarn at hand in case you need to mend something.

Dyeing Wool on Your Own

You only need a little time and patience to dye your wool in your favorite color. Dyeing uses only natural dyes.

Dyeing with Plants

We need a large enamel pot, a few wooden spoons, a thermometer, a kitchen scale, a measuring cup, vinegar, and a hotplate for coloring with plants. Pure wool and pure silk are best for dyeing with plants. However, since each tissue reacts differently to the color or absorbs it differently, it is always recommended to carry out a sample first. Before dying, the dyed material to be dyed should be weighed since its weight is relevant for the pickling at the later chemical level. The dye solution should never come into contact with metal; the pot should also be large so that the wool has enough space in it. Always use wooden spoons to stir. Otherwise, the wool will become tangled.

Before the wool is dyed, it must be pickled for color picking. The required stain, such as iron or copper sulfate, is available in every pharmacy. For this purpose, the pot is filled with water, and the mordant should be added so that it dissolves. We squeeze out the previously softened wool in water and place it in the slightly warmed pickling bath. At 50 to 65° C, the whole is then well-stirred for 45 to 60 minutes. Then, the wool is taken out and rinsed out.

For dyeing, the shredded dry plants are placed in a pot with plenty of water and heated. A little later, we add the wool. The temperature should be slowly increased to 90 to 95° C. For 50 to 60 minutes, we let this draw while we all stir. Over two wooden spoons, we drain the wool, shake off the plant parts, and rinse the wool in lukewarm water. Finally, we squeeze the wool into a mild detergent solution, rinse it, and add a dash of vinegar to the final rinse water before hanging it out to dry or into a well-ventilated room.

Color Selection

- We achieve yellow shades through birch or coltsfoot leaves, as well as through St. John's wort or chamomile.
- Green is best obtained by using Iceland moss, earth smoke, or oak leaves.

- We get light and dark brown colors by using flowers from heather or walnut leaves when dyeing.
- Using the madder root as a colorant, we get a red hue.
- Orange is created by over-dyeing a yellow color with madder again.
- We achieve blue with indigo.
- We can create a gray-green hue by over-coloring the yellows with indigo.

- We get strong violet tones when we dye reds with indigo.

Chapter 3. Types of Crochet

1. Amigurumi Crochet

Amigurumi crochet is a crochet art form that originated in Japan, and it refers to the creation of small, stuffed toys or creatures produced using sewed or crocheted yarn. Ami implies crochet or weave, and Kigurumi implies a stuffed doll. If you ever observe a little doll or toy produced using yarn, that is amigurumi.

Things to make utilizing the amigurumi kind of crochet:

– Children's toys

– Larger novelty pads and homewares

– Fan things

2. Aran Crochet

Refers to ribbed or cabled crochet. It's traditionally Celtic style crochet with interlocking cables and can make thick beanies, sweaters, and scarves. Aran is also a load of yarn, so be wary of that when you read the word 'Iran' in a pattern. At the point when you see a picture of somebody snuggled under a major, comfortable-looking blanket – that is Iran.

Cro-Hook

Cro-Hook is a variation of Tunisian crochet. Similar techniques and stitches are utilized in both of these kinds of crochet. However, Cro-Hook utilizes a double-finished crochet snare, called a cro-snare, making it possible to work from the two parts of the bargains with two colors. Pretty incredible.

Numerous names also know this kind of crochet. Here's a couple:

• Cro-Hook

• Cro-Knit

• Cro-Knitting

• Double Hook Crochet

• Double-Ended Crochet

• Double-Ended Tunisian

• Crochet as soon as possible

Since you can utilize two colors without a moment's delay, you can make a two-sided fabric. That implies that if two colors are utilized, one side of the fabric is one color, while another side is predominantly the subsequent color.

For this reason, it's an enjoyment strategy to use for scarves, where the two sides appear. It gives your project a reversible impact. It's also great for afghans. At the point when you have one side up, it's one color. At that point, flip it over, and it's a different color.

3. Bavarian Crochet.

Bavarian crochet is another crochet type, and this is a vintage crochet stitch that is customarily work in adjusts like granny squares. It makes a thick texture and considers mixed shading changes instead of sharp shading changes like with granny square. Every region is worked in two sections – a base row of bunches and a row of shells chipped away at the top. Bavarian crochet looks like extremely unrestrained granny squares.

Things to make using the Bavarian kind of crochet

4. Bosnian Crochet

Bosnian crochet causes a thick, to sew like texture using just the crochet slip join, worked in various pieces of a fasten from the last row. You can buy Bosnian crochet snares; be that as it may, it can likewise be worked with normal crochet snares. It's additionally now and again called Shepherd's weaving. IT likewise looks an extensive sum, such as sewing. It's not presently an extremely well-known style, and in case you see it, you'll presumably trust it's sewn.

5. Bullion Crochet

A specialized crochet stitch is accomplished with a mix of yarn wraps around a very long snare, forming a particular and one of a kind 'roll' stitch. Bullion crochet is usually utilized for themes rather than fabric-based projects. It results in a thick, uniform, round theme style piece.

– Stiff things like placemats

– Motifs for decoration

Things to make utilizing the Bullion sort of crochet

6. Broomstick Crochet

It is vintage crochet fasten that is added to a great extent called jiffy ribbon, and it's made with a daily crochet catch, yet the lines are conformed to something long and wide like a broomstick handle. Most current crocheters use huge crochet snares or thick dowel to do broomstick ribbons these days. Broomstick trim is an amazing crochet ability to learn, and it brings about an exceptionally lovely and unique last item.

Things to make using the Broomstick kind of crochet

– Delicate shawls

– Throw covers for adornment

7. Bruges Crochet

This technique is used to make Bruges trim – where 'strips' of crochet are made and afterward crocheted together to shape complicated ribbon patterns. Most grandmothers have some high-quality Bruges style crochet things disguised in drawers and enveloped by destructive verification paper.

– Intricate shawls

– Embellishments for clothing

– Tablemats

Things to make utilizing the Bruges sort of crochet

8. Clothesline Crochet

It is a crochet style where the conventional join is placed over a thick rope length of thick twine to make round mats and cartons that hold their shape. That is normally seen as a preliminary technique and can be followed back to Nepal and Africa's craftspeople.

Things to make using the Clothesline kind of crochet:

– Baskets

– Mats

– Structural tapestries

9. Clones Lace Crochet

This crochet style is intensely connected to Irish trim crochet and was made because it was much faster and simpler to make than needlepoint ribbon. The Clones tie is a piece of the clones crochet range of abilities. Clones trimmed an extremely down to earth crochet style and were used for practical purposes during wars.

Things to make using the clones ribbon sort of crochet

– Openwork scarves

– Delicate dresses and tops

10. Cro-catch Crochet

Cro-catch crochet is worked with a twofold completed catch to make twofold sided crocheted. It permits the crocheter to work lines on or off either end of their crochet piece and to have neither a set-in-stone side to what they're chipping away at. This is likewise sometimes called Cro-sew. This style is like Tunisian and results in fantastic colorwork that isn't attainable in different crochet styles.

11. Filet Crochet

This is a crochet style made with chains and twofold crochet. It's a lattice-like pattern where squares are either filled or not occupied, and the negative space is used to take pictures inside the piece. The remarkable thing about filet crochet is that you can embed pictures using the texture's full and void squares.

Things to make using the filet sort of crochet

– Baby covers

– Jackets and kimonos

– Hand sacks

– Cushions

12. Finger Crochet

Fundamentally, finger weaving, finger crochet is similar to crocheting, just without the catch! It's a type of hand texture weaving in the style of crochet lines. Finger crochet is fun when you're starting, be that as it may, as the finished strain is free, you'll presumably need to continue ahead to a catch before long and make increasingly adaptable ventures.

Things to make utilizing the finger kind of crochet:

— Simple string sacks

— Basic scarves

13. Freeform Crochet

Freeform crochet, otherwise called Freestyle crochet, is a mix of everything without exception crochet. There's also no set pattern to follow. You can start with a couple of stitches or a small theme and then add other stitches or pieces to it in any capacity you'd like. You're creating your project by utilizing the stitches and pieces you love in any capacity you like.

Working without a pattern is why such a significant number of people love this kind of crochet; however, it very well may be very scary to numerous others on the flip side of that.

However, it really shouldn't be because freeform crochet allows you to join all the stitches and techniques you love into a beautiful bit of artwork.

This kind of crochet is regularly used to make themes and appliques, yet it can also create clothing, scarves, sacks, or anything you need.

Most of the freeform crochet you'll see is worked in numerous colors for a bright, striking look. It tends to be worked in all a similar color, however, for a marvelous completed look. Whenever utilized with the right yarn, it can bring out the different textures and stand out.

Things to make utilizing the freeform kind of crochet

— One-off clothing times

— Art pieces

14. Hairpin Crochet

This is similar to broomstick crochet, aside from that, it's worked with a traditional crochet snare with the crochet piece held educated between two thin metal rods. A while ago, when this strategy was created, actual metal hairpins were utilized, which got its name. This style results in an extraordinary completed fabric.

15. Micro Crochet.

Micro crochet is another type, this type is a modern crochet style, and it's accomplished utilizing very fine thread and extremely fine crochet hooks. This is a very tasking work and probably best for more patient crocheters.

Things to make utilizing the micro sort of crochet

– Teeny minor things

– Embellishments

– Talisman

16. Overlay Crochet

A crochet base is made, and stitches are included top to create a raised pattern. This opens up numerous possibilities for beautiful and intricate colorwork.

Things to make utilizing the overlay sort of crochet

– Potholders

– Wall hangings

– Hand packs

17. Pineapple Crochet

This isn't such a lot of a procedure, and it's more of a general stitch and shape pattern. You can utilize pineapples in crochet, cause doilies, scarves, and in any event, clothing. When you realize how to recognize a crochet pineapple, you start seeing them everywhere. This is a stitch style that was popularized during the 70s.

Things to make utilizing the pineapple sort of crochet

– Dresses

– Tops

– Shawls

– Wraps

18. Recolored glass crochet

Very similar to overlay crochet. However, the top part is usually done in black yarn to create a contrast-colored glass influence — a kind and striking crochet style.

Things to make utilizing the recolored glass sort of crochet

– Thick, sturdy things

– Winter scarves

– Handbags

19. Symbol crochet

It is otherwise called diagram crochet and is well known in Japanese fasten books. It's a valuable ability to learn as you can get any image crochet book in any language and do the activities using the graph. Note: Your life will change once you figure out how to crochet from image patterns.

Things to make using the symbol kind of crochet

– Complicated patterns that are hard to clarify in words

– Foreign language patterns

20. Tapestry Crochet

It is the crochet equivalent of colorwork. It's also called intarsia crochet. There is a wide range of strategies for working in tapestry crochet, and each style gives different results. Tapestry crochet is one of the numerous approaches to do colorwork.

Things to make utilizing the tapestry sort of crochet

– Color workpieces

– Imagery based plans

21. Tunisian Crochet

Since you work on a long snare with a stopper toward the end or a snare with a cord connection, Tunisian crochet is very similar to knitting in that you have many live loops at some random time, and you work your loops on and off your snare, much the same as in knitting.

22. Hairpin Lace Crochet.

The Hairpin crochet is also known as Hairpin Lace, is a system that creates loops on the two sides of worked crochet stitches. This strategy makes strips (or braids) of lace. At that point, the loops on the strip are crocheted or braided together, creating a beautiful lace project.

Originally, actual metal hairpins were utilized for this strategy, which is the way it got its name. It was very famous in the Victorian era when elegance and magnificence indicated wealth and stature.

The hairpin crochet is presently worked utilizing a loom, usually called a hairpin lace tool or hairpin loom. The loom normally has two metal rods, called prongs, associated with plastic bars on end. There are different holes in the plastic bars with the goal that you can alter the size of your loops.

The yarn or string is contorted around the prongs of the loom, making the circles. Crochet lines are then worked down the center to hold the circles set up. This outcome in a portion of the ribbon with circles on either side of the fastens.

A fundamental strip, which most patterns use somehow, is made with single crochet down the middle. When you learn this procedure, it's very simple.

23. Irish Crochet

The Irish crochet is a lace style of thread crochside a short period, here, you may learn how to make crochet chain in a short time and a slip stitch to starting some of your projects, and then you have to know at any rate one fundamental stitch. Before long, you'll have a scarf, cap, shawl, or a blanket.

Chapter 4. Mastering the Basics

Now that you have the tools and ideas for crochet projects and may have found some patterns to try out, you may come across many things you don't understand. There are some steps to the pattern that you are not familiar with, and that's okay. You will learn them here and now.

Let's first learn the basics of crochet.

Making a Slipknot

To start almost any crochet or knitting project, you will need to make a slipknot. You will need to follow several very easy steps. First, you will take the yarn and choose where you want the slipknot to be placed. Some patterns require leaving a very long tail because of casting on stitches or maybe because you may need it to sew together some pieces, etc. You should check the pattern to see how long the tail should be.

Once you decide that, you will make a loop with your right-hand yarn attached to the yarn ball on top of the tail part of the yarn. You will hold the loop between your index finger and your thumb of your left hand and take the yarn with your right hand, and put it through the loop, creating another loop that was pulled through the first one. Lastly, you will hold the knot and pull the second loop until it tightens the knot. This way, you have made a slipknot that is counted as the first stitch in knitting.

You can tighten it once you insert a needle through the loop by pulling the tail. Another way to do this is by taking the yarn and wrapping it around your index finger twice. Then you will take the lower loop and pull it above the upper loop. Now, all you have to do is take the lower loop (that used to be the upper) and place it on your needle. Tighten the slipknot once you insert the needle by pulling either side of the yarn.

1.

2.

3.

4.  **5.**  **6.**

Chain Stitch (CH)

Now that you have made a slipknot, you will need to chain some stitches. The process is very easy, but you need to relax and not pull the yarn too tight because it will only become more difficult for you to work the stitches. However, you don't want to loosen the yarn too much because your work will lose the structure. Keep it tight, but not too tight. You'll understand once you get started. You can practice by chaining hundreds of stitches; it's not that hard nor time-consuming as one would think.

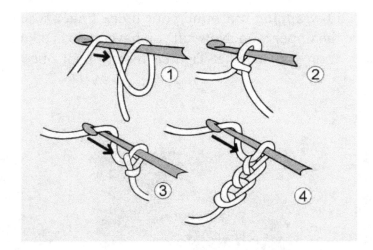

So, to make a chain stitch, you will first need to make a slipknot, and then, holding your crochet hook with a slipknot in your right hand, you will take the yarn using the hook, not from your tail, but the rest of the yarn ball and pull it through the loop. You will repeat this as many times the pattern calls for. As I said, it is very easy and basic.

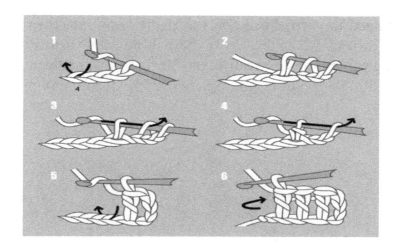

Single Crochet Stitch (SC)

Once you have your chain, you can start working different stitches into the chain. One of the basic stitches is the single crochet stitch. It is also very easy to do; just follow the instructions.

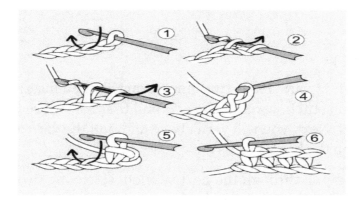

To make this stitch, you will insert the hook into the center of the following working chain and take the yarn using your hook and pull it through the chain stitch. This way, you will have two loops on your hook.

Double Crochet Stitch (DC)

To make the double crochet stitch, you need to yarn above and then insert the hook into the center of the following working chain and yarn above again. Then, you will pull the yarn through the chain stitch. You will yarn above and pull the yarn through the first two loops, leaving only two loops on your hook. You will then yarn above and pull through both of the loops, creating a double crochet stitch. You will repeat these steps as many times it is required in your pattern.

Half-double Crochet Stitch (HDC)

To make this stitch, you need to yarn above and insert the hook into the center of the following working chain stitch and yarn above again. Next, you will pull the yarn through the chain stitch, which will result in having three loops on your hook. Next, you will yarn above and pull the yarn through all three loops, creating one half-double crochet stitch. Of course, you will repeat these steps as many times as necessary.

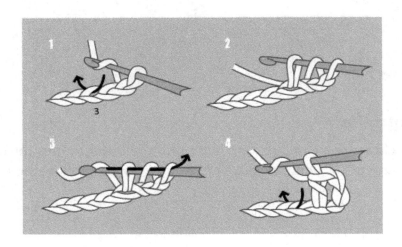

Triple Crochet Stitch (TC)

To make this stitch, you will first yarn above two times. You will then insert the hook into the center of the following working chain stitch, yarn above, and pull the yarn above the chain stitch. You will have four loops on your hook. Next, you will yarn above and pull the yarn above the first two loops, parting three loops in total on the hook

You will then yarn above and pull through the next two loops, leaving two loops on the hook. And finally, you will yarn above once more and pull the yarn above the both of the loops, creating a triple crochet stitch or a treble. You will repeat these steps as many times as necessary to complete the pattern.

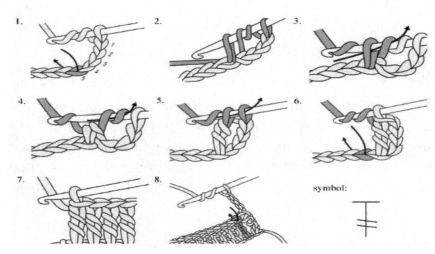

If you followed the instructions carefully, you probably have succeeded in creating the stitches. However, that is just the beginning. Those stitches are just the basics, the ones that will be helpful in your later work. But there are many more that you will find to be very exciting and fun to make. And you will learn them here. Continue reading and creating...

Shell Stitch

When it comes to the shell stitch, there are many variations, and the pattern will usually give instructions on how to make that exact shell stitch, but if you are feeling creative and want to create something on your own and would like to use shell stitch, but you don't know how to do it, here's how!

To create the shell stitch, you will make multiple chains of six stitches, or if you want to use the stitch as an edging, you will count in sixes for the number of shells you will make, and you will add one more chain. The first two chains from the hook will count as one double crochet (dc). Then, you will work five dc into the third chain

The set of five dc creates the shell effect. To secure the first shell, you will skip two chain stitches and work a single crochet (sc) into the chain stitch after. So, to complete the row, you will repeat the following: skip two stitches, work five dc into the third stitch, skip two stitches, and work a sc into the sixth stitch. You will repeat this until the end of the row, ending with a sc. If you work only one row of sc, it will make a wonderful edging, but you can also work in multiple rows and create something bigger, like a blanket or a pillowcase.

Treble Shell Stitch

This one is very similar to the previous one, only that the shells are much bigger and bolder. It can also be used for borders or crocheted in rows for some other purposes. To create this stitch, you will work in a series of eight stitches for each shell, and you are going to add three more stitches.

So, you will work a half-double crochet stitch (hdc) into the hook's third chain in the first row. You will then repeat the following for every shell you will make: skip three chain stitches and work seven triple crochet stitches (tc) in the fourth chain stitch. You will then skip the following three stitches and work an hdc stitch into the eighth chain stitch. You will repeat this as many times as required.

For the second row, you will chain four and turn your work. The chain four will count as the first tc in this row. You will work three more tc into the same stitch to create half of the shell. Then, you will work a hdc stitch into the center of the shell from the previous row. Next, you will work seven tc into the next hdc from the previous row.

You will repeat this until the end of the row, i.e., you will crochet a dc in the center of a shell from the previous row and a shell of seven tc into the hdc stitch from the previous row. When you reach the end of the row, you will work a hdc into the last shell and work four tc into the last hdc from the previous row to create another half of the shell.

In the third row, you will chain two and turn your work. Then, you will work a hdc in the first stitch. You will then repeat the following: Work seven tc into the next hdc and a hdc into the shell center. You will then finish the row by working seven tc into the last hdc stitch and a hdc into the chain from the beginning of the previous round. To make this a pattern, you will repeat the second and the third row until you reach the desired length.

Lace Shell Stitch

Another variation of shell stitch that can be used for many different things is this one. It is nice and airy, and it will look adorable on anything. You will need a series of eight stitches, plus three more. So, if you start with a chain, chain multiples of eight stitches and add three more; if you are changing your pattern into shell stitches, then count the stitches in multiples of eight. To make this stitch, you will need to repeat the following for each of the shells: one tc, chain one, one tc, chain one, one tc, chain one, one tc. All of these are worked into the same stitch to create the shell effect. So, to make a shell pattern, you will chain in multiples of eight, plus three more stitches.

Then, you will crochet a hdc stitch into the third chain from the hook. Then, you will skip three chains and work the lace shell into the fourth stitch. You will then skip the following three chain stitches and work a hdc stitch into the eighth chain stitch. You will repeat this all across the row. In the second row, you will chain four and turn your work. The chain will count as one tc. You will work one more tc into the same stitch, chain one, and work another tc into the same stitch.

You will then repeat working hdc stitches in the center of the shells from the previous row, and you will work shells into hdc stitches from the previous row. When you reach the end of the row, you will crochet a hdc into the last shell center and then work one tc, chain one and then work two more tc into the same stitch. In the third row, you will chain two and turn your work. You will crochet a hdc into the first stitch. You will then repeat what you did in the previous row, i.e., you will work lace shells into the hdc stitches and hdc stitches into the center of each lace shell from the previous row.

You will end the row with a lace shell in the last hdc and work a hdc stitch into the chain from the beginning of the previous row. You will repeat the second and the third row until you reach the desired length.

Puff Stitch

This stitch is the one that looks great but feels even better. Of course, there are many variations of the stitch, but it will look gorgeous whatever you make. The pattern is perfect for blankets and scarves, but you are free to use it for whatever your crocheting hands lead you to.

To make a simple puff stitch, you will work incomplete hdc stitches. That means that you will yarn above, insert the hook into the stitch, yarn above, pull the yarn through the stitch, and instead of completing the stitch by pulling the yarn through all three loops; you will yarn above again and insert the hook into the same stitch, yarn above and pull the yarn through the stitch.

You will do this once more so that you will have seven loops of yarn on your hook. Then you will carefully yarn above and pull the yarn above all seven loops. To secure the stitch, you will need to chain one. To make a pattern out of a puff stitch, you will need to chain multiples of two and add four more stitches. In the first row, you will work a puff stitch into the fourth chain from the hook. Then, you will chain one and skip the next chain stitch. You will then repeat the following pattern until the end of the row: puff stitch, chain one, and skip the following chain stitch. You should finish the row with a puff stitch.

Then, you will chain three and turn your work. Next, you will work a puff stitch in each chain one space and chain one in between the stitches. You will do this across the row, ending the row with a puff stitch in the chain from the previous row's beginning. You will repeat this process until you reach the desired length.

Basic V Stitch

The V stitch is a very basic stitch with an amazing texture and is very easy and quick to make. It consists of two dc stitches, separated by a chain stitch.

To make a pattern out of the V stitch, you will need to chain multiples of three and add seven more stitches. To make a V stitch, you need to work one dc stitch, one chain stitch, and one more dc stitch into the same chain stitch. After you crochet the foundation chain, you will work a dc stitch into the fourth chain stitch from the hook. The three chains will count as the first dc in the row and one chain as a separation. So, to continue, you will chain one and skip the next chain.

You will then work one dc in the next chain stitch, chain one, and another dc into the same chain and skip the next two chains. You will repeat this until you reach the end of the row. When you reach the end of the row, you will chain one, skip the next two chain stitches and work one dc in each of the following two chain stitches. Then, you will chain three and turn your work.

The chain will count as the first dc in the row. Then you will work a dc into the next dc stitch. Next, you will chain one and work one V stitch into each of the V stitches from the previous row. Then, you will chain one, skip the next chain stitch and work one dc stitch into each of the last two dc stitches. You will repeat the second row until you reach the desired length.

V Stitch Bricks

This stitch is a blend between a V stitch and a granny square pattern. It is done in rows, like V stitch would generally be done; the only difference is that it is done in the spaces between the Vs. and not on top of each other.

So, to make a pattern using this combination, you will chain in multiples of four-plus nine more stitches. First, you will work a dc stitch into the fourth chain stitch from the hook. You will then repeat the following: chain one, skip the following three chain stitches, work a V stitch in the fourth chain stitch. You will repeat this until you reach the end of the row. Then, you will chain one, skip three chains, and work one dc into each of the last two chain stitches.

In the second row, you will chain two and turn. You will then work dc stitch into the next dc, chain three, and skip the first chain and the first V stitch. You will then work V stitches in the spaces between the V stitches from the previous row and chain one between the V stitches. You will repeat this until the end of the row. Then, you will crochet one more V stitch, chain three, skip the next V stitch, work one dc in the next dc and one dc in the chain from the beginning of the previous row.

In the third row, you will chain two and turn around the work. You will then work a dc in the next dc, chain one, and work a V stitch in the following space. You will then repeat the following: chain one, crochet a V stitch in the space between the V stitches from the previous row. You will do this until you reach the end of the row.

Moss Stitch

This stitch is also known as granite stitch. It is very easy to do, as it requires you to know only the chain stitch and the single crochet stitch.

To begin, you will need to crochet an odd number of chain stitches. You can place a marker in the first chain stitch from the hook, just to keep track of where you need to work your stitches. Once you get the hang of it, you can stop using the marker. So, having placed the marker, you can continue with the work. You will crochet a sc stitch into the third chain from the hook. Then, you will repeat the following sequence: chain one, skip the next chain, work a sc stitch into the next chain stitch. Repeat until the end of the row.

Chain one and turn your work. In the second row, you will work sc stitches into each chain one space and separate them by chain one. You will repeat this until the end of the row, where you will work a sc stitch into the chain stitch where you have placed the marker, removing it before crocheting the stitch.

Chapter 5. Terms and Vocabulary

This is a basic skill that all beginners must master. If you can read and understand patterns, you open up a whole new world and create possibilities.

In this chapter, we'll take a step-by-step look at the basic patterns to help you understand how to read and process them.

Check the type of yarn you need, the amount of yarn, hook size, and gauge. Find the special stitches or instructions required for the pattern.

Next, look at the actual patterns to make sure you understand the stitches and how they work together.

If you find any stitches you don't know, look at one resource or written instruction to guide you through the stitching.

US	UK
The chain(ch)	The chain(ch)
The single crochet(sc)	The double crochet(dc)
The half double crochet(hdc)	The half treble(htr)
The double crochet(dc)	The treble(tr)
The treble crochet(trc)	The double treble crochet(dtr)

Make sure you pay attention to the terms used before purchasing patterns.

Reading crochet patterns can be fairly time-consuming at first, but you'll get used to it. Patterns are written in rows for items that are straight and flat, such as a square cloth. For something like a coaster, the pattern is written in rounds, which is the terminology we use.

Here is a row to practice reading:

- Row 1: Chain 12, dc in 2nd chain from the hook and across in each. Chain 1, turn (9)

Firstly, you can see that this is part of a straight, flat item pattern because it refers to row 1. Next, chain 12 indicates that this is a chain made up of 12 chain stitches.

After this, there will be the half double crochet in chain number two from the hook (excluding the one carried by the hook). The half double crochet follows this in each stitch till the end of the row. Then you'll make one chain stitch for the following row.

Ready to try another one? This time we'll look at using asterisks. Here we'll focus on what part of the pattern needs to be repeated. Leave a piece of long thread, chain 21. Sc in the second chain and each across. (20 sts) - approximately 5" wide

Row 1: *single crochet in first st, double crochet in the next* repeat till the end. Chain 1 and turn (20 stitches)

Leave a long piece of yarn, then start your chain, which will be 21 stitches long. Next, make a single crochet in the second Ch stitch from the hook (exclude the stitch with the hook) and single crochet in each chain until the end of the row. It should be approximately 10 inches wide.

In row one, read the pattern carefully. You'll notice that there are only two asterisks. Everything in between the asterisks needs to get repeated till where the row ends. Firstly, the single crochet is done in the first stitch; then, the double crochet is what follows in the next. A single crochet in the first stitch comes again and is then followed by the double crochet. Follow through till the row ends. Make one chain stitch so that you can begin a new row.

This is just one example; you will learn as you go along. In addition to reading written patterns, you will also be able to use symbols to read patterns. Below is an elaborate list of common crochet symbols that are commonly used.

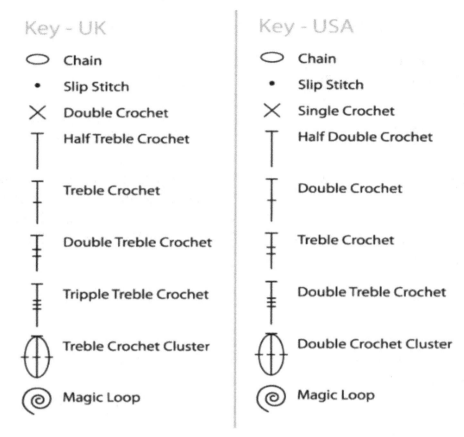

Key - UK

◯ Chain

• Slip Stitch

✕ Double Crochet

Half Treble Crochet

Treble Crochet

Double Treble Crochet

Tripple Treble Crochet

Treble Crochet Cluster

Magic Loop

Key - USA

◯ Chain

• Slip Stitch

✕ Single Crochet

Half Double Crochet

Double Crochet

Treble Crochet

Double Treble Crochet

Double Crochet Cluster

Magic Loop

ABBREVIATIONS

ch = chain; hdc = half double crochet; st(s) = stitch(es).

FINISHING

Sew buttons to opposite ends of rows with buttonholes.

Weave in ends.

Chapter 6. Crochet Pattern Techniques

Crochet with Plastic Rings

Pure fun brings crocheting with plastic rings. A brisk job that brings results quickly. However, you should not crochet the rings individually but create coherent chains.

Making a Crochet Ring

To start, put the normal crochet start loop on the plastic ring. The loop for the first solid ash and all subsequent hands is always pulled through the ring. Then, as usual, the two loops that are on the needle are embraced with an envelope. Repeat this until the ring is completely crocheted. Before you start work, crochet a ring completely to the sample to know how many units are needed above all. That is also dependent on wool strength.

Connect Rings

The connection between two rings occurs when the first plastic ring is crocheted in half with solid hands. Now, crochet an air mesh and then the first solid mesh around the next ring.

The last ring of a row is always completely crocheted. All other half-finished crocheted rings will be completed in the second round with solid hands. In doing so, always crochet a solid piece of ash around the connecting air mesh. In the end, pull the thread through the last stitch and sew it.

The second row of rings can now be half crocheted and connected to the first row's rings. When crocheting the first half of the second row of rings, add the already finished first row of rings. To do this, crochet a slip stitch into the middle stitch of the already finished ring row.

The crochet with plastic rings is particularly suitable for original placemats, small coasters, and fabric bags, which receive special design. Of course, all these suggestions are also suitable for individual gifts.

Crochet Flowers

These flowers are crocheted with wool for a crochet hook of strength 4 in rounds, and each of them is closed with a Kettmasche.

- Close the chain of 6 meshes with a chain stitch to the ring.
- 1st round: 12 fixed sts.

- 2nd round: in every M. 2 tr. (Replace the first trump with 3 ch.).
- 3rd round: Instead of the first tr. 3 ch., Then into the first st. 1 tr., In the next M. Crochet 1 tr and 1 half tr

* At the following 4 m. in each puncture site 1 solid st., 1 half st. And 1 st., then 2 st., in the 4. Crochet 1 tr and 1 half tr. *

Repeat 4 times and replace the 6th sheet with 1 solid M., 1 complete half tr. and 1 tr. Cut the thread and pull it through. You can combine several individual motifs into one flower or stitch together two individual motifs in different colors. Thus, simple blankets and crocheted with raffia, even carpets.

Tunisian Crochet

The characteristic of the Tunisian crochet is that the picture on the front and back is different. Also, the mice can hardly stretch. Unlike "normal" crocheting, you have all the hands of a row on the needle here. These are summarized in a first step and then mended in a second step. The needle is held like a knitting needle. Choose a crochet hook that is long and has a uniformly thick shaft. You can crochet Tunisian with wool and synthetic yarns.

- **Step 1:** The basis is an air chain, which has to be crocheted loosely. The loops are to be taken, as shown in the picture. You always start at the right edge of the crochet work.
- **Step 2:** In the next step, knit the loop on the left edge with an envelope. After that, two slings are always embarrassed. When the last two loops are cut off, the first row is finished. Many styles of Tunisian crocheting arise with such two steps: grasping and chopping.
- **Step 3:** For the subsequent rows, grasp the loops, as shown in the figure below, from the vertical mesh wires. The stitching of these loops takes place, as described in step 2.
- **Step 4:** When you finish the work, the last row's loops must be chained off. To do this, crochet a warp stitch in the vertical wire of each machine.

Chapter 7. Crochet Stitches

You need to practice the basic stitches and memorize the different crochet terminologies to create your masterpiece. Although you can always look in this book for a quick reference on the stitch you must use, it is more comfortable to crochet if you've memorized how to do a certain stitch.

In this chapter, you will learn how to make some simple-complicated stitches. You will also encounter some of the crochet terms in their abbreviated form so you can practice your crochet language.

Picot Stitch

Some patterns use "p" to symbolize a picot stitch. Picots are used to add decoration to a pattern and sometimes as fillers.

On the area where you're planning to add a picot stitch, do three chain stitches. Insert your hook into the third chain from your loop. Sl st to close the stitch.

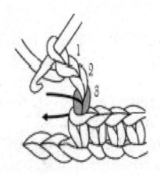
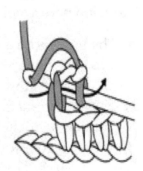

Add the picot stitches to the areas where you need to put them.

Cluster Stitch

Cluster stitch has no known abbreviation, but some patterns go with "cl" as the cluster's abbreviation. A cluster usually forms a triangle.

To best illustrate, you will need dc stitches to make a cluster. You must leave each of the two remaining loops open in the first 3 dcs.

- To start, yarn over and insert your hook through the next stitch. Make your first dc, but when you only have two remaining loops on your hook, don't slip the thread through the remaining two loops. Leave the loops hanging from your hook, and you'd end up with one unfinished dc.

- Yarn over and insert your hook into the next stitch to make your second dc. Now, you have four loops on your hook.

- Yarn over and slip the thread through the first two loops of your second dc. At this point, you have 3 loops on your hook. Leave them hanging from your hook. You should have 2 unfinished dc stitches.

- Do the same with the remaining dc stitches you need to make to create your cluster stitch.

- At this point, you should have 4 unfinished dc stitches.

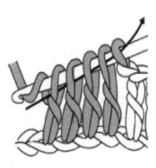

- Yarn over, then slip the thread through the 5 loops on your hook, and you will produce 1 dc cluster.

Popcorn Stitch

This stitch is named as such because it does look like one. A popcorn stitch is a rounded and compact stitch that pops out. You can place your popcorn stitch in front or back – it all depends on the effect you want to achieve in your piece.

- In making a popcorn stitch, you need 5 dc together in one stitch.

- Remove your hook from your current loop; make sure not to lose the current loop and just drop it in the meantime.

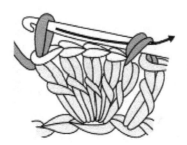

- Insert your hook in front (as shown) of the first dc in the group if you want to pop your stitch in front. Insert your hook from the back if you want it to pop at the back.

- Hook your dropped loop and let it slip through the dc stitch to get a popcorn stitch.

- V-stitches resemble the letter V, hence the name. You can crochet loosely using this stitch, especially if you want to create lacy designs. You can also make your stitches tight and compressed.

- To begin, do a dc, ch 1, and another dc on the same stitch. In between the two stitches, the single ch st separates the two dcs (to resemble the letter "V"). Keep in mind that the two dcs should be on the same stitch.

Shell Stitch

The shell stitch is an adaptable crochet stitch and comes in different variations.

- To begin, do dc 4 on the same stitch. You should be able to come up with an inverted cluster. A shell stitch is easier to do than a cluster stitch. You can close each dc immediately, and you don't need to wait for the last dc to close the stitch.

Puff Stitch

The puff stitches create a different texture to your work. This stitch follows the same procedure as the cluster, but you need to place all the dc stitches in the same stitch. You also need to work on 3 dc stitches to create one puff stitch.

- To start, make a dc stitch and leave the last two loops open or hanging. You should have one unfinished dc stitch on your hook.

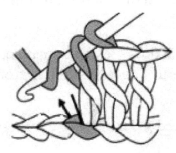

- Start with your second dc stitch on the same stitch as the first unfinished dc. Leave the three loops hanging from your hook.

- Now, begin your third and last dc for your puff stitch and bring it together with the first two dc stitches on the same spot. Yarn over, then slip the thread through the first two loops, and you will have four loops hanging on your hook. Yarn over, then slip the thread through the four remaining loops, and you will get a dc puff stitch.

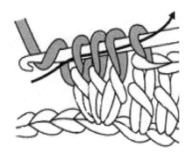

Are you ready to try some patterns?

Tapestry Crochet

Tapestry in the round is the most common way to work tapestry crochet.

This example is using single crochet.

-Start with a round of stitches.

-Hold the new yarn color behind your work and simply crochet over this new color a few stitches to secure it

-Stitch before where you want to use your new color, insert into the upcoming stitch, but yarn over with the new color, and pull through as normal

-The new color stitch work as your normal stitch, but this time work over the yarn tail from the original color.

-Repeat this same process when you want to switch back to the original color.

-Stitch before you want to use your original color, insert into the upcoming stitch, but yarn over with the original color, and pull through as normal.

-The original color stitch work as your normal stitch, but this time work over the yarn tail from the new color.

Surface Slip Stitch

-Start with a field of crochet stitches; this example is single crochet.

-Insert your hook from top to bottom through the work you'd like to start the surface crochet stitches.

-From the bottom, take the yarn for surface crochet, make a loop over the crochet hook, and gently pull through the work.

Pull through a loop from the yarn's working end, and then pull through the work like a slip stitch through the other loop.

-Continue in the desired pattern.

Working in Rows

In short, this simply means working back and forth from one side to the other.

You will want to rely on your pattern here because it will tell you how many to chain. For this example, we will use a single crochet.

-Let's say your pattern asked you to chain 10:

-You will then single crochet in the first chain from the hook and all the following chains:

-Now turn your work and chain 1:

-Now single crochet in all stitches, starting with the 2nd stitch from the hook; unless directed otherwise by the pattern:

Working in Rounds

In short, it simply means that you will be working in a circle.

You will want to rely on your pattern here because it will tell you how many to chain.

-Chain the required number of chains:

-Connect the first and last stitch with a slip stitch. This will form a ring:

-In the first round, you will crochet into each stitch unless directed by the pattern:

-Slip stitch the last stitch and the first stitch together to finish up each round.

-To start your next round chain (we are chaining one for single crochet) and chain all the way around. Finish with a slip stitch to connect:

Switching Colors

-Insert the crochet hook into the upcoming stitch and then yarn over:

- Gently pull the yarn through only one loop on the crochet hook.

-Now release the loose end of the original color of yarn and hold the new color yarn against the piece of work:

-Yarn over the crochet hook with the new color of yarn that you have selected:

-Gently pull the new color of yarn through the remaining 2 loops left on the crochet hook

-Now, with the new color of yarn, continue your pattern as directed:

Chapter 8. Easy Beginner Patterns

Ribbed Boot Cuffs

- Yarn
- Yarn needle
- 5.50   mm/ I hook

Instructions

- **Gauge**: 14 st x 17 r = 4" in back loop single crochet (blsc)
- Ch 19
- **Row 1**: Single crochet in the second chain from your hook and in each chain stitch across (18)
- **Row 2**: Chain 1, turn and back single loop crochet in each stitch across (18)
- Repeat row 2 until the piece measures 8" across (without being stretched) or until you achieve your desired length.
- Ch 1 and insert the hook through the 1st stitch on both edges, then slip stitch to join the boot cuff's edges.
- Repeat procedure down the side. Cut the yarn and weave in the ends. Repeat to make the other boot cuff.

Leg Warmers

- 6 mm crochet hook
- 2-3 skeins
- Darning needle
- Scissors

Instructions

- Ch 35
- Join with a slip stitch to the 1st chain. Ensure that your chain is not twisted.
- **Row 1**: Chain 3 and double crochet into each chain, then join to the 3rd chain with a slip stitch.
- **Row 2-28**: Chain 3 and double crochet into each stitch. Join the third chain with a slip stitch.
- Bind off and weave in the ends.

Crochet Washcloth

Crochet Coffee Sleeve

- Chunky yarn
- 9mm N hook

Instructions

- **Row 1**: Chain 20 and slip stitch to join
- **Rows 2-5**: Chain 1 then half double crochet across the 20 stitches, and slip stitch to join
- **Row 6**: Single crochet across and weave in the ends.

Blanket Scarf

- 11.5 mm hook
- 318-424 Yards of Bulky size 6 yarn

Instructions

- **Gauge**: 6 stitches x 4 rows = 4×4 square
- **Length**: 52 inches without the fringe

- o **Row 1**: Chain 28, then double crochet into the second chain until the last chain stitch, chain 2, then turn.
- o **Row 2**: Double crochet across, chain 2 and turn.
- o Repeat row 2 for 45 rows or until you achieve your desired length.
- o Finish off at the end of your last row and weave in ends.

Crochet Face Scrubbies

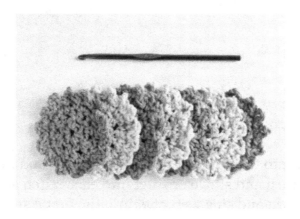

- ▪ Yarn needle
- ▪ 5mm crochet hook
- ▪ Worsted weight cotton yarn

Instructions

- o Chain 4 and join with a slip stitch to create a ring.
- o **Row 1**: Chain 2, then single crochet into the center. (Chain 1 and single crochet into the center) Repeat 4 times. Chain 2 then join to the 1st stitch with a slip stitch; you should now have a total of 12 stitches around the circle.
- o **Row 2:** Chain 2 (half double crochet 2 times into the gap from the previous round, chain 1) Repeat 5 times. Half double crochet into the gap formed from the previous round. Ch 1 then join into the 1st stitch with a slip stitch; you should now have 18 stitches around the circle.
- o **Row 3**: Chain 2 (single crochet, chain 1). Repeat 8 times. Single crochet 2, then join to the 1st stitch with a slip stitch; 27 stitches around the circle.
- o **Row 4:** Chain 1 (chain 3 and slip stitch into the next stitch, sc) Repeat 12 times. Chain 3 then slip stitch in the final stitch.
- o Secure the final stitch, then weave in the ends with a yarn needle.

Washcloth Set Crochet Pattern

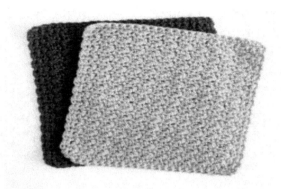

Instructions

- o Approximate dimensions 9.5" by 9.5."
- o **Gauge:** 2"= 5.5 single crochet
- o Ch 26
- o **Row 1**: Single crochet into the 2nd chain from your hook and into each stitch across.
- o **Row 2**: Chain 1, then turn and single crochet into each stitch across.
- o **Row 3**: Chain 1, then turn and single crochet into the first 2 stitches. *single crochet into the next stitch, then double crochet into the following stitch; repeat from * across then single crochet into the last 3 stitches.
- o **Row 4**: Chain 1, then turn. Single crochet into the 1st stitch *single crochet into the next stitch, then double crochet into the following stitch; repeat from * across then single crochet into the last 2 stitches.
- o **Row 5-29**: repeat rows 3 and 4.
- o **Row 30-31**: Chain 1, then turn. Single crochet into each stitch across
- o Cut the yarn ad tie it off. Weave in all ends.

Men's Crochet Scarf

- Light worsted weight wool yarn
- 6.5 mm hook

Instructions

- 16 stitches and 28 rows = 4inches in pattern
- Approximate dimensions = 75" by 5"
- Chain 301 (use stitch markers to mark every 25 stitches to keep track of the chain stitches since they are quite many).
- **Row 1**: Slip stitch into the second chain from your hook, and in each chain, stitch across the row (300 slip stitches).
- **Row 2**: Chain 1, then turn. Work on the entire row with slip stitches (300 slip stitches).
- **Row 3**: Chain 1, then turn. Work on the entire row with slip stitches (300 slip stitches)
- **Row 4**: Chain 1, then turn. Work on the entire row with single crochet (300 single crochet stitches)
- **Row 5**: Chain 1, then turn. Work in slip stitches for the entire row in front loop only of the single crochet from the row below (300 slip stitches)
- **Row 6**: Chain 1, then turn. Work in slip stitches for the entire row (300 slip stitches)
- **Row 7**: Chain 1, then turn. Work in slip stitches for the entire row (300 slip stitches)
- **Row 8**: Chain 1, then turn. Work in single crochet for the entire row (300 single crochet stitches)
- Repeat rows 5-8 until you achieve your desired scarf length. Ensure you end with 3 slip stitches rows
- End off, then weave in the ends.

Mug Rugs

- Yarn needle
- 5 mm crochet hook
- 4.25 mm crochet hook
- 1 skein worsted weight cotton yarn
- Scissors

Instructions

- Main coaster
- **Row 1**: Chain 8, single crochet in the second chain from your hook and in the following 6 chains (7 single crochet stitches).
- **Row 2**: Chain 1 (doesn't count as a stitch through the entire project), single crochet in the 1st stitch, and each stitch across (7 single crochet stitches).
- **Row 3-9**: Repeat row 2, then knot off and cut the yarn.
- Fringe ends
- Cut 14 4" pieces of yarn. Take one piece of the yarn and fold it in half to attach the fringe. Insert into a stitch using a crochet hook and pull up the cut piece. Bring the cut ends through the loop and pull until tight. Repeat across in every stitch on both ends, then trim the ends to match.

Crochet Dishcloth

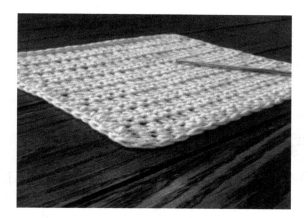

- 1 skein cotton yarn
- I hook

Instructions

- o Chain 25
- o **Row 1**: Into the 3rd chain from your hook, half double crochet until the end of the foundation chain – you should now have 22 stitches across. Chain 2 and turn.
- o **Row 2:** Half double crochet 22 times, chain 2, then turn. Continue until you have 16 rows – don't fasten off.
- o Add a single crochet row all around the 4 sides of your cloth. Begin by putting one single crochet in the stitch you are working on now. Rotate the cloth to crochet down the left side.
- o Single crochet in each space down the side - It does not need to be exact; just ensure it is even as you go down; otherwise, your cloth will bunch.

Crochet Ear Warmer

- 5.00 mm hook

- Tapestry needle
- Scissors
- Worsted weight yarn

Instructions

- Chain 56
- **Row 1**: Slip stitch into the first chain.
- **Row 2**: Start working in rounds; chain 1 and half double crochet around, then join to the first half double crochet.
- Repeat row 2 until you have 8 rows – you can add more if desired.
- Fasten off and leave a long tail.
- To cinch the ear warmer, thread the tail into your yarn needle. Collect the seamed section of your headband and fold it into half, ensuring that the fold is facing you.
- Bring either of the sides to the top of your fold and secure it in place.
- Run the needle through all the sections of the material you have gathered.
- Wrap your yarn around the underside of your cinch, then through the sections once more. Do this several times to secure the cinch, fasten the end and weave in the tail.

Color Block Bag

- Darning needle
- Scissors
- Light worsted yarn- 3 colors
- 5.00 mm hook
- 4 metal D-rings

Instructions

- Ch 54 with color A

- o **Row 1**: Single crochet into the 2nd chain from your hook and single crochet into every stitch across the row and chain 1.
- o **Row 2-4**: Single crochet in every stitch across the row, then chain 1 and turn
- o **Row 5-18**: Single crochet, double crochet into the 1st stitch, skip a stitch, *single crochet, double crochet into the following stitch, skip a stitch * repeat* to the end - end with a single crochet in the last stitch. Chain 1 and turn.
- o **Row 19-36**: Change to color B. Single crochet then double crochet into the 1st stitch, skip a stitch, *single crochet then double crochet into the following stitch, skip a stitch *repeat* to the end, ending with a single crochet in the final stitch. Chain 1 and turn
- o **Row 37-75**: Change to color C. Single crochet then double crochet into the 1st stitch, skip a stitch, *single crochet then double crochet into the following stitch, skip a stitch *repeat* to the end, ending with a single crochet in the final stitch. Chain 1 and turn.
- o **Row 76-92**: Change to color B. Single crochet then double crochet into the 1st stitch, skip a stitch, *single crochet then double crochet into the following stitch, skip a stitch *repeat* to the end, ending with a single crochet in the final stitch. Chain 1 and turn
- o **Row 93-106**: Change to color A. Single crochet then double crochet into the 1st stitch, skip a stitch, *single crochet then double crochet into the following stitch, skip a stitch *repeat* to the end, ending with a single crochet in the final stitch. Chain 1 and turn
- o **Row 107-110**: Single crochet in each stitch across the row.
- o Cut the yarn and weave in the ends.

Fall Crochet Bunting

- ▪ Size 4 yarn in two colors
- ▪ 6.0 mm hook
- ▪ Scissors
- ▪ Yarn needle

Instructions

- o **Gauge**: 4" across= 13 double crochet
- o **Approximate dimensions**: Each rectangle = 6.25" tall x 4.5 " wide

Crochet Pillow

- ▪ Bulky weight yarn
- ▪ 6.5 mm crochet hook
- ▪ Scissors
- ▪ 18" pillow insert
- ▪ Yarn needle

Instructions

- o **Row 1 (RS):** Chain 48 – first 2 chains count as 1 double crochet, 1 double crochet in the third chain from your hook, and in every chain across (47 dc)
- o **Row 2:** Chain 2 and turn, 1 front post double crochet into each stitch across – 47Front post double crochet.
- o **Row 3:** Chain 2 (counts as 1 double crochet) and turn, 1 double crochet in every stitch across – 47 double crochet.
- o **Row 4-31:** Repeat rows 2 to 3
- o **Row 32:** Repeat row 2
- o Fasten off the 1st piece after row 32. Don't fasten off the 2nd piece after row 32.

Finishing

- With the wrong sides touching, hold the 2 pieces together. Proceeding from where you left off at the end of row 32 on the 2nd piece:
- Chain 1, single crochet evenly around 3 sides going through both pieces, insert the pillow insert, and proceed along the 4th side. Invisible join to the first single crochet and fasten off.

Barefoot Sandals

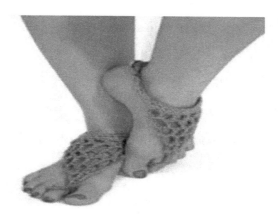

They're so cute! Imagine you are going to the beach or swimming pool, and you are wearing your own handmade and barefoot sandals. You can pin these colors to match your mood and attire. First, you can make an ankle strap and then create a triangular shape of sandals sewn to the center of the three spaces' first chain by sliding. This will naturally reduce the line until you form a point in your thumb. Before crochet, the initial loop glides the yarn button, and when the crochet is made. When knitting a button opening, it puts it in the right position.

The gauge is not important for this project.

You will need a ball of lion brand micro-spinning in lavender and size G/6 (4mm) crochet and tapestry needles, woven at the end.

Note: If the piece is too long, the leg skips line 8 through the working slip to the center of the second place on the row, then runs on line 9.

Chain 6 is associated with a slip seam, forming a button aperture loop.

Line 1: Chain 36, sliding button-down and away at the end of the line, single crochet in the second chain from the hook and cross to the ring for the strap on the ankle, end of crochet in the second chain from the hook, and across to the ankle strap ring end-35 pins.

Line 2: The last pin on the front loop, the 11th pin, one crochet connects the yarn with one crochet, the next loop 14 PIN-15 pins.

Line 3: Chain 6 (counting DC and chain 3 space), Skip 1 pin, DC in the next stitch, chain 3, span-8 DC, and 7 circuit space.

Line 4: Slip to the center of the first chain 3 space, chain 6 (counting DC and chain 3 space), DC in the center of the chain 3 space, (Chain 3, DC in the lower circuit 3 space) through, leaving the remaining stitches do not work-7 DC and 6 chain Space.

Line 5: Repeat lines 4-6 DC and 5 chain space.

Line 6: Repeat lines 4-5 DC and 4 chain space.

Line 7: Repeat lines 4-4 DC and 3 chain space.

Line 8: Slip to the center of the first Circuit 3 space, chain 3 (Countdown DC), DC in the center under the chain 3 space twice-3 DC.

Line 9: First PIN-slip, central DC single crochet.

Line 10: Twist, one crochet in one crochet.

Line 11: Bend, single crochet in one crochet, chain 8, slip pin in the same crochet for toe ring, end.

Chapter 9. Home Décor Styles

Horizontal Buttonhole

For this example, we are using single crochet. However, you would use this same technique with other stitches.

-First Row: Work your stitches in to where the buttonhole will be. You will, then, skin the number of stitches needed for the diameter of the buttonhole. Chain the number of stitches that you skipped. For this example, we skipped 5, so we chained 5. After you chain, continue the row of the first stitch after the stitches you skipped:

-Second Row: You will crochet the regular pattern across the row over the chain stitches. You will then continue working your pattern as directed:

Loop buttonhole

We are using a single crochet; however, you would use this same technique with other stitches.

-You will begin this on the last row or while you are edging.

-Find where you would like to have your buttonhole. Skip the number of stitches so that it equals the correct diameter for the button. You will then chain the same number of stitches that you skipped. For this example, we skipped 5, so we chained 5.

-Turn the work over make sure that the chain is doubled back. Then slip stitch into the last stitch; in this case, the last stitch is a single crochet.

-Now, single crochet over each of the chains. Tip: The piece's integrity needs to have the exact number of single crochets as you have chains.

-To finish off the loop, simply slip stitch over the next stitch and continue to the pattern as directed.

Backstitch Seam Joining

-Start by holding the two pieces of work right sides together. To keep them steady, you may want to tack them together while you work. You will need a darning needle to backstitch, and you will work from right to left:

- Insert the darning needle straight through the work from the top piece of work to the bottom.

- Then reinsert the darning needle from the bottom to top in stitch 2 ahead:

- Then insert the darning needle where your last stitch ended; Each stitch will be worked halfway through the previous stitch. You will continue the previous technique until you reach the end of the row:

Tip: This may result in a bulky thick seam.

Granny Square Joining

-To start, make sure that you know the order you would like the squares to appear in your blanket.

-Stack the squares in order so you can keep track of which square belongs in each part of the blanket. For example, if you have 80 squares, you will want ten stacks of 8 squares.

Remove the top square from a stack, set it on the left of the stack, then take the next square and set it to the right of the first square you removed from the original stack.

-Put these two squares together with the backs touching one another.

-Chain 3 in the very corner of the front/top square (Square A).

-Now make 3 double crochet trebles in the corner of the bottom square (Square B)/

-Now 3 double crochet trebles in the upcoming space of Square A.

-Then 3 double crochet trebles in the upcoming space of Square B.

-Continue this method until you've reached the bottom of the two squares. Then in the bottom corner space of Square B, make one double crochet treble.

-Bind off.

-Continue this method with the rest of the squares in the stack.

-Once you have all your short rows complete, we move onto the next phase, joining the rows of squares.

-Lay the rows with the backs facing one another.

-Then, repeat the previous pattern to combine the rows.

-You'll end with a single, double crochet treble in the final corner space.

Join as You Go with Granny Squares

This method works great if you want to join your granny squares without having to sew them all together at the end.

-Start in a corner. When you come up to the next corner, make a granny cluster of 3 tr. You will then need to locate what square this new square will attach to.

-Make a chain as you normally would with a corner. For the second chain, insert the crochet hook from front to back to catch the corner of the square you are attaching to. Pull through the corner and then through the loop.

-Now make a chain without joining.

-Make the second 3tr granny cluster in the corner. To join the other square, repeat the joining method in each space between the granny clusters: Make a chain as you normally would with a corner. For the second chain, insert the crochet hook from front to back to catch the corner of the square you are attaching to. Pull through the corner and then through the loop.

-A tip for this corner is to attach to the top and side squares, not the corner square. Insert the crochet hook front to the back to grab the top square corner's yarn, gently pull through the corner and the loop. This is your 1st chain that normally appears in the corner. Make a chain, but don't join. Insert the crochet hook front to the back to grab the side square corner's yarn, gently pull through the corner and the loop. Then make the 3 tr cluster in the corner and continue to join to the side square as you did above: Make a chain as you normally would with a corner. For the second chain, insert the crochet hook from front to back to catch the corner of the square you are attaching to. Pull through the corner and then through the loop.

-The final corner is joined by chaining, joining, and chaining as you did before.

Needle Overcasting Joining

-Start by holding the two pieces of work right sides together. To keep them steady, you may want to tack them together while you work. You will work from left to right:

-You will insert the needle through both layers of fabric:

-Then, bring the needle overtop the work and insert through the work from the same side as before:

-Repeat this technique until you reach the end of the work:

Tip: This technique will give you a less polished look but a less bulky finish.

Whip Stitch Joining

-You will need a needle and a long length of yarn for this method.

-Begin with the right side of two squares facing one another.

-Start in the corner of the two squares.

-Pull the needle through matching stitches of each square. Leave about 6 inches.

-Reinsert the needle into the same stitch and secure the stitch by placing it through the 6-inch loop and tightening.

-Continue this method until all squares are combined.

-Make sure to weave your tails of yarn into the work to hide it.

Tip: Start with joining squares into rows and then joining the rows together.

Crochet Hook Joining

-Start by holding the two pieces of work right sides together. To keep them steady, you may want to tack them together while you work:

-You will begin joining by inserting the crochet hook into the top strands of the first stitch in each piece of work:

-Yarn over, gently pull through, and chain 1:

-Continue the preceding technique for each stitch until you reach the end of your work:

Chapter 10.   The Most Common Mistakes

There is barely anything more crippling than looking down at your crochet venture and understanding that it takes a gander at all like your pattern. However, everybody submits blunders, and even the most experienced crocheter becomes adjusted to pulling that yarn to unwind her work a portion of the time.

It turns out there are simple approaches to solve all the most well-known mistakes you can make in crochet. Continue reading to learn how to solve these setbacks:

1. Not reading the pattern

It's all too easy even to consider plunging into an enticing new project without reading through the pattern properly, at that point realizing, past the point of no return, that you missed a stage or need more yarn on hand. Before starting, pause for a minute to familiarize yourself with all the instructions, and you'll be vastly improved prepared for whatever surprises the pattern has in store.

2. Utilizing the wrong yarn

Now and again, it's very enticing to plow through a project utilizing a different yarn than the pattern indicates. While you don't need to purchase the specific brand listed, you should always try to get a similar yarn load.

You may figure, what amount could it matter if you use fingering weight yarn rather than thick? The answer is, there could be sufficient differences to ruin the completed impact.

If you attempt to make a thick winter scarf with a sensitive two-employ yarn, you'll get an exceptionally odd effect. Similarly, an unimposing napkin pattern crocheted with a massive yarn will give you an awkward finished article, and any confounded will be hard to execute with thick yarn.

If you would prefer not to go out and purchase yarn for each new project, it's a smart thought always to coordinate the project to the yarn you have on hand, not the other path around.

3. Utilizing the wrong snare size

So, you don't have a great right snare for your project? You have, say, a B/1 snare, and the pattern calls for a D/3? Will it have any kind of effect? The answer is very likely, yes. The bigger the difference between the snare the pattern requires and the one you're utilizing, the greater the possibility that you'll spoil the final look of your project.

On the off chance that your snare is one size out, you can probably pull off it, contingent upon the pattern, yet a large hole between the required size and whatever you have in your hand implies the final result will likely be either a lot smaller or larger than indicated.

With certain projects, this doesn't make a difference. If, for example, you are making an Afghan blanket and all your squares turn out to be four crawls rather than 2.5 inches, at that point, it is anything but a problem; your bigger snare will give you a bigger blanket at last, which is fine as long as that is OK with you. Utilizing a smaller or larger snare will result in the proportions of the sweater or cardigan getting distorted.

So, the rule is, get the correct catch if you're making something where the inevitable size of the piece truly matters to you. A simple answer to this is to get many measured snares. The set available here accompanies 11 different sizes.

4. Crocheting too tightly

Crocheting also tightly is a slip-up that we as a whole make toward the start of our adventures with crochet. It's usually brought about by clutching the yarn too tightly and wrapping it too enthusiastically around the snare. As you become more a professional, your crocheting will relax, and the clustered pressure of your early projects will turn into a relic of times gone by. Remember not to yank the yarn and hold it loosely when wrapping it around the snare to facilitate your crochet.

5. Not making a strain square

Numerous patterns request that you make a speedy strain square before you start a project. They will determine a certain number of stitches per row for the project, and you should focus on that. All the size calculations in the pattern have been made based on this size of stitching.

At the point when you're a beginner, sitting around when you're biting the dust to continue ahead with your pet project can appear to be ridiculous. I've frequently thought myself, "Goodness, I don't have to bother with that," and at that point, further down the line, I've realized that my sweater or cardigan isn't turning out very right. The reason is incorrect pressure since I didn't complete that little square right toward the start.

So truly, causing a strain square can appear to be a period squandering annoyance, yet it is regularly vital. On the off chance that the pattern requests one, it's probably because the measurements are easy to get wrong on the project, and the designer needs to spare you the far greater disturbance of unraveling half a sleeve further down the line. Make the strain square. It spares time at last.

6. Mixing up U.S. and U.K. terminology

It's easy to start breezily crocheting a pattern and then realize things aren't exactly working out because you're utilizing U.K. terminology rather than the U.S., or the other way around. Most patterns will indicate whether they're utilizing American or English terms, or they'll place the alternative name for a stitch in brackets. However, to be safe, here's a really useful conversion chart:

7. Not including the number of stitches

Most patterns will include the number of stitches in a row in brackets, and they'll also state what number of rows are expected to make up the project. Usually, rows are fairly easy to check, contingent upon the pattern, and stitches are also on the off chance that you look closely. Keeping a consider you come can help you avoid any terrible surprises when you're polishing off. Make this easier on yourself by having a pen and paper near when you're crocheting and taking note of down numbers as you go.

8. Losing or picking up stitches

It's normal to crochet happily along, only to suddenly see that your work has gone lopsided. I've done this so often with scarves, where any mistakes in checking rows or stitches leap out. At the point when you lose or gain stitches, the problem is that you're not forming your turning chain (necessary when you turn over the work to do another row), or you're splitting the yarn with the snare and then working a similar bit of yarn twice. The two problems are easy to sort out once you've seen them. However, the most straightforward approach to correct them is by unraveling. So, watch out for your rows as you work them, and inquire whether they are even as you come. Remember to tally up those stitches.

9. Not blocking the project

Few out of every odd project needs blocking, yet anything you need to have a crisp, flawless, professional completion will profit from this process. If you are making squares for an afghan, for example, your final product will be a lot more pleasing on the off chance that you wet and peg out your work.

10. Not completing the project

Some of the time, your crochet turns out to be a lot more complicated or tedious than you first envisioned, and it tends to be enticing to lay it aside for a while and start something different or simply abandon it entirely. If you've contributed time and effort — and cash — it's always worthwhile persevering. All crocheters commit errors, yet we as a whole improve, as well, and regardless of whether it takes you ages to get a completed result, you'll still be proud when you complete that last stitch. At the point when your family compliments you on your lovely project, you'll feel that special glow that originates from a vocation well done.

Chapter 11.   Secrets to Be a Better Crocheter

Adding Accents to Your Creations

Now that you know how to create all kinds of different projects, I want to go over how you can add different accents such as flowers to your projects.

First, we will learn how to make a flower by itself; then, we will discuss what you can do with that knowledge.

To begin making a flower, you need to start with a slipknot. Then chain seven and then go back to the first chain stitch you created and push your hook through it. Yarn over and pull through the chain stitch and the loop on your hook, leaving yourself with one loop on the hook.

This will create your slipstitch. You will have a small circle now with a hole in the middle. It is that hole that we are going to work into to create a flower.

Now you want to create a chain of four. Now we are going to work on a triple crochet stitch. First, yarn over twice so you will end up with three loops on your hook.

Now put your hook into the hole that we created in the center of the flower, yarn over, and pull through this will leave four loops on your hook. Yarn over and pull through two loops. This will leave three loops on your hook. Yarn over and pull through two loops, leaving you with two loops, then yarn over and pull through the last two loops.

You will repeat this step, yarn over your hook twice, put the hook through the center hole, hook the yarn's working end, and pull through. Yarn over and pull through two, yarn over pull through two more, and yarn over pull through the last two loops.

Do one more of the triple crochet stitches into the hole in the center of the flower. Then chain four. To finish the first petal, you will push your hook through the center hole, not yarning over just the hook. Hook the yarn's working end, pull it through, and then pull that loop through the loop on your hook without doing anything else.

Now you are ready to create the next petal, chain four, and then create three triple crochet stitches into the flower center. Create a chain four and do another slip stitch.

You are ready for the third petal, so chain four, and create three triple crochets through the flower center, chain four followed by a slipstitch.

Follow the same directions for creating the fourth, fifth, and sixth petals. Depending on the size of your hook and your yarn, you may be able to add even more petals. When you get to the end of your last petal, chain four, create a slip stitch, and cut your yarn. Make sure you pull it tight, so it does not unravel.

Depending on the number of petals, you created your flower should look something like this.

Next, we will learn how to create a beautiful 3D crochet rose.

The first thing you want to do is create your slipknot. For this, you want to chain 60, so this will be a fairly large rose. You want to keep your chain stitches fairly loose; this will create the rose much easier down the line.

Once you have finished your 60 chain, add three more chains. Yarn over and insert your hook in the fourth chain from the hook. Yarn over and pull through; this will leave you with three loops on your hook. Yarn over, pull through two, yarn over, and pull through the final two loops completing a double crochet stitch.

For the rest of this row, you want to add one double crochet into each stitch on your chain. After you have double crocheted down the row, go ahead and turn your work. This is one instance where you will not create a chain stitch before turning in your work.

Yarn over and skip one stitch. Instead of inserting your hook in the middle of the stitch, you will insert it under both loops of the stitch or the V. Yarn over and pull through. You will now have three loops on your hook. Finish this just like you would a double crochet stitch. Yarn over, pull through two loops, yarn over and pull through the remaining two loops.

Going into the same stitch, you want to do 7 more double crochets, so you have a total of 8 double crochets in that stitch. Once you have completed this, you will skip a stitch and complete a single crochet under the V of the next stitch.

Skip one stitch, and under the next V, you will create eight more double crochet stitches.

Skip one stitch and under the V of the next stitch, create a single crochet. You are going to continue this pattern down this row.

This is what your project will look like at this point.

Once you have finished this row, you want to tie it off because that is the end of this project's crocheting! All you have to do now is take one end of your project and start wrapping it into a rose.

Once you have the rose wrapped the way you want it, you need to take your yarn needle and thread it either with the tail you left when you stopped working or with another piece of yarn. Sew into the bottom of the rose, attaching all of the layers so that it does not come apart. Depending on how you wrapped your rose, it should look something like this.

Now, this is a pretty large rose, about the size of the palm of your hand. After you have created it, you can do with it to add these to throws, hats, scarfs, or any other project by using your yarn needle to sew them on.

You can create so many things with crochet that your imagination is literally what will limit you. You can make tons of different flowers, hearts, patterns, and so many different projects.

I know, at the beginning, it may seem a bit overwhelming, but don't let yourself get stressed out while you are crocheting; the entire point of art is to relax and create something beautiful. I promise you that if you allow yourself to get frustrated, you will not create something beautiful.

The next thing we are going to learn is how to make a bow. The first thing you will need to do is to create your slipknot. Next, you will create a chain of 22. Once you have created your chain of 22 turns, you project and work an entire row of single crochet stitches.

At the end of this row, chain one and turn your project and work another single crochet row. Chain one, turn your work, make a third row of single crochet stitches, and continue with a fourth row.

Next, you will take both of your ends and fold them together, so they line up. You will find loops on the ends, and using one loop from each end, you will connect the ends.

Push your hook through the two loops, yarn over and pull through the first two loops, yarn over again and pull through the last two loops creating a double crochet stitch. You will continue with the double crochet stitches down the ends.

Make sure you get the very last stitch on end so it is connected evenly. Once it is connected, you will remove your hook, take the loop and the tail and tie both in a knot leaving your working yarn out of the knot. Push the knot as close to the project as possible and cut.

Turn the project inside out and make sure the seam is in the middle of the back. Now take a small piece of yarn, wrap it around the middle of the bow and tie it twice, making sure it is in the bow center. Now you will wrap the yarn around the bow as many times as you would like, tie it twice in the back, cut the yarn, and now you have a bow.

You can add this bow to headbands, hats, or even slip a bobby pin through the back to make a hair bow. If you want to make a larger bow, you will start with more chain stitches and add more single crochet stitching rows.

Of course, you can change the bow up as I did in the picture using two different colors of yarn or even creating a chain stitch to wrap around the middle instead of just the yarn. Whatever you do is going to make the bow your very own creation.

The last accent I want to go over with you is a heart. For this project, you are going to be using a magic circle. To do this, you need to take the end of your yarn in your dominant hand and wrap it around the index and middle finger of your other hand toward you two times.

Take your hook, push it under both loops on your fingers, hook the back loop, pull it under the front loop, then yarn over with the yarn's working end and pull through. This can be awkward at first, but it will get easier. Gripping your loop on your hook with your right hand, slide the loop off your index and middle finger. Yarn over, insert your hook through the large loop, yarn over, and pull through.

Yarn over again, pull through two loops, and yarn over, pull through the last two loops creating a double crochet.

Next, you will need five triple crochet stitches. To do this, you will yarn over twice, insert your hook into the large loop, yarn over pull through, yarn over, pull through two, yarn over pull through two, and yarn over pull through the last two. Do not worry that your large loop is too big; we will deal with it later. Just make sure you do not make it too small.

Do this four more times working into the large loop. Once you have completed this, you need to work four double crochet stitches into the loop.

Ensure that you do not pull on your tail while working and do not work it into your project; you must keep the tail separate.

Next, you will chain 2. That will create the point of your heart. Now you will be making the same stitches you did before but in reverse order, so double crochet four times into your loop. Followed by five triple crochet stitches.

Work one double crochet stitch into the loop, and we will finish off with a slipstitch. To create a slip stitch, insert your hook through the loop, hook your working yarn, pull it through the loop and then pull that loop through the loop that is on your hook.

Leave you hook in your work, grab your tail and pull it. You will see your heart take shape. Sometimes it can take a little bit of pulling to close up the center. Just make sure you don't break your yarn. Once your center is closed up, you will see the completed heart. At this point, you can cut your working end, and you have created a cute crochet heart in less than 10 minutes.

Chapter 12.   Basic Washing Instructions

Yarn and wool, which are the two most common fibers used in crochet and knitting, can be particularly tricky to wash and take care of because of how fragile they are. If it is done incorrectly, then all of your hard work on your project could be ruined by either miss-shaping, discoloration, or shrinking, which is why you should always follow any specific washing instructions that come with your wool.

For example, recycled yarn, organic natural wool, or yarn you make yourself generally has not undergone any treatments and needs to be dealt with correctly first to destroy any pests or bacteria that can linger. Those that haven't been chemically treated will not be suitable for sensitive skin without thoroughly washing first.

Hand Washing

Generally speaking, yarn or wool is hand washed to avoid damaging the yarn. For articles or projects that are quite long, such as socks or scarves, handwashing avoids them becoming too stretched, which can happen during the machine's spin cycle (see below).

Hand washing is incredibly simple once you know how and all you need is:

- Lukewarm water
- Wool wash or specific hand wash detergent (to avoid aggravating your hands)
- Bucket/Sink
- Towels

Method:

1. Fill the bucket and add a ratio of 1 Tablespoon of detergent/wash to 1.5 Litres of water.

2. Mix it thoroughly until the detergent has diluted in the water.

3. Press your projects into the water so that the water seeps into all of the fibers in the yarn or wool.

4. Move the project article around in the water and make sure it is completely immersed in the water and leave it for 15-20 minutes to soak.

5. Drain the water out and rinse the detergent out thoroughly (with wool wash, you don't have to rinse, follow the instructions that come with it), alternating pressing some of the water out and rinsing again. Make sure not to wring or stretch out the yarn/wool or you could miss-shape it.

To Dry:

1. Press out as much water as you can and place the article on a dry towel.

2. Roll up the towel and press down on it, which will remove even more water.

3. Hang and air dry until they are ready to use again.

Hand washing doesn't always do the trick in today's modern times because more spills, messes, and stains (especially projects relating to children or pets) mean you must use a machine to disinfect or get a cleaner finished project. Also, for regularly worn articles that may need more frequent washing, you will find using a machine is easier and more time-effective.

Top Care Machine Tips

Here are some basic tips that you should know about cleaning your yarn that is a general guideline to start if you have nothing specific for your skeins or wool stash.

No "vigorous" washing – This means ensure that you keep the spin cycle low and that you do not wring out the project after you have washed it. This is because yarn and wool tend to lose their slight elasticity when it is wet, which means that when it is rung out or thrown in a high spin cycle, it can become stretched and ruin your project's fit.

Wash below 40 degrees – Avoid hot washes where possible because the heat can miss-shape the yarn as well as shrink your project. In addition to this, on very hot washes, it can even cause the wool or yarn to harden as if it were burnt, which can cause scratching on the skin if worn.

Non-bio only – for those with sensitive skin, children, and pets, it is best to use non-biological washing powder, which is softer on the skin and less likely to cause irritation or discomfort (especially on projects have to be worn). This is because the biological components can sometimes linger in the yarn's fibers and cause skin rashes or irritation for those who have frequent contact.

Re-Shape when wet – To avoid the wool or yarn from having kinks or losing its shape permanently, you should make sure that you gently re-shape the project before hanging to drip dry. You can use gravity to help straighten your project if you are hanging from a line (make sure not to damage the project with pegs/hooks)

Minimum Amount of Fabric softener – This qualifies for other chemical washing components as well that can not only linger and cause skin irritation in a similar way to the washing powder, but the chemicals in fabric softener can react with any dyed wool or yarns, which means there can be some discoloration or stripping your project of all of its color.

Steam iron – Many believe that you can't iron yarn or wool as it can singe the edges and make them hard and coarse. However, this is not the case; using an iron on a steam setting and spraying with water beforehand should protect your projects from the heat of an iron. Alternatively, if you don't have a steam setting, you can put the iron on a low heat and use a damp tea cloth or towel and iron to protect the project's fibers.

No Tumble Drying – The best way to avoid damaging your projects (particularly shrinking or burning) is to avoid tumble drying altogether, which can burn (and in some cases catch fire if left long enough) the project. If you decide to tumble dry anyway, be wary of the static electricity and sparking risk after the cycle and avoid spraying any aerosols near the room when unloading the washing.

Fundamentally the key point to remember is to avoid heat on the yarn where possible, which is the most likely cause of damage to projects.

Conclusion

Congratulations on purchasing this Crotchet book, and thank you for doing so.

Before you start crocheting, you have to consider a series of tips that will make your life as a weaver much easier than you think. As you go above the needles and find a position that is comfortable for you to wear the strand when knitting, you will gradually relax, let go of the knitting, and find your own "tension of weaver."

When you start crocheting, it is often so overwhelming that the wool escapes between your fingers, the needles are drained, and the stitches are released while crocheting. This insecurity that causes us to face something new makes us weave the point very tightly. It's normal for this to happen, and you don't have to get overwhelmed or give it a lot of importance. You're not going to weave that tight always.

But until that happens, it is advisable to start crocheting with the right needles. So, what are the right needles when you start? The first thing you should know is that there are no good needles or bad needles in themselves. In principle, each type of needle is designed for fiber and a type of weaver.

But when you start for the first time, you have to keep in mind that the needles offer some resistance and make them "break" the stitches on them a bit. This will make it harder for you to slip the needle's stitches and escape it, giving you better control over what you are doing. And for this, the needles that offer more resistance are bamboo.

Therefore, when you start crocheting, it is good that you start with this type of needles so that you can knit more comfortably. But as you learn, it is ideal to try different types of needles.

The first time you will try, and since you have never done it until now, your first instinct is a color that you can combine well with your clothes. I don't know why this happens, but the first thing that comes to mind is to choose dark wool (black, brown, navy blue, etc.), thinking that we can give more use to what we are going to weave because we can combine it better with our closet bottom.

I hope this book gave you the inspiration you need to start crocheting and take the skills you have learned here and show them off to the world. As with any new craft, practice makes perfect, and the more you work at this, the better you are going to become.